# Minnesota

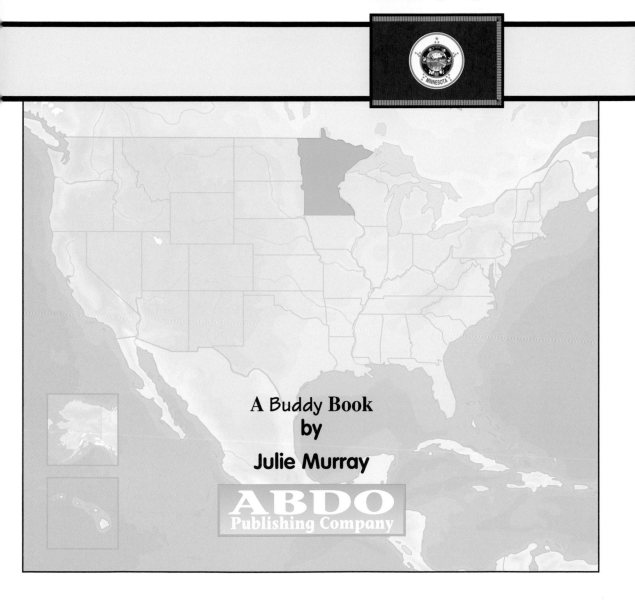

A Buddy Book
by
Julie Murray

**ABDO**
Publishing Company

## VISIT US AT
### www.abdopub.com

Published by ABDO Publishing Company, 4940 Viking Drive, Edina, Minnesota 55435.

Edited by: Sarah Tieck
Contributing Editor: Michael P. Goecke
Graphic Design: Deb Coldiron, Maria Hosley
Image Research: Sarah Tieck
Photographs: Brand X Pictures, Camp Snoopy pictures courtesy of Bob Cole, Chris Gregerson of cgstock.com, Clipart.com, Digital Vision, Getty Images, Mall of America, Minden Pictures, One Mile Up, PhotoDisc, Scenic Photo!, Underwater Adventures picture courtesy of Underwater Adventures Aquarium

### Library of Congress Cataloging-in-Publication Data

Murray, Julie, 1969-
    Minnesota / Julie Murray.
        p. cm. — (The United States)
    Includes index.
    Contents: A snapshot of Minnesota — Where is Minnesota? — All about Minnesota — Cities and the capital — Famous citizens — Fort Snelling — Outdoor fun — Mall of America — A history of Minnesota.
    ISBN 1-59197-682-0
        1. Minnesota—Juvenile literature. I. Title.

F606.3.M87 2005
977.6—dc22

                                    2005043335

# Table Of Contents

# A Snapshot Of Minnesota

Minnesota's landscape includes rolling hills, high bluffs, wooded forests, and rich farmland. But, when people think of Minnesota, they think of water. Even this state's name means water. Minnesota's name comes from a Native American word. It means "sky-tinted waters."

Minnesota is sometimes called the "Land of 10,000 Lakes."

There are 50 states in the United States. Every state is different. Every state has an official state nickname. Minnesota is sometimes called "The Gopher State." This refers to small animals named gophers that live on prairies in the southwestern parts of the state.

Gophers live on Minnesota's prairies.

Minnesota became the 32nd state on May 11, 1858. It is the 12th-largest state in the United States. It has 84,397 square miles (218,587 sq km). It is home to 4,919,479 people.

# Where Is Minnesota?

There are four parts of the United States. Each part is called a region. Each region is in a different area of the country. The United States Census Bureau says the four regions are the Northeast, the South, the Midwest, and the West.

# Four Regions of the United States of America

ALASKA

WASHINGTON
OREGON
MONTANA
IDAHO
WYOMING
NEVADA
CALIFORNIA
UTAH
COLORADO
ARIZONA
NEW MEXICO

NORTH DAKOTA
SOUTH DAKOTA
NEBRASKA
KANSAS
MINNESOTA
WISCONSIN
IOWA
MISSOURI
MICHIGAN
ILLINOIS
INDIANA
OHIO

OKLAHOMA
TEXAS
ARKANSAS
LOUISIANA
MISSISSIPPI
ALABAMA
TENNESSEE
KENTUCKY
WEST VIRGINIA
VIRGINIA
NORTH CAROLINA
SOUTH CAROLINA
GEORGIA
FLORIDA

VERMONT
MAINE
NEW HAMPSHIRE
MASSACHUSETTS
NEW YORK
RHODE ISLAND
CONNECTICUT
PENNSYLVANIA
NEW JERSEY
DELAWARE
Washington D.C.
MARYLAND

HAWAII

West    Midwest    South    Northeast

Minnesota is in the Midwest region of the United States. It is the largest state in the region. People living in Minnesota experience many different types of weather.

People fish on frozen lakes in Minnesota. This is called ice fishing.

Minnesota has four seasons. These seasons are spring, summer, fall, and winter. It is cool in spring and fall, and cold and snowy during winter. During summer it is hot and humid. Hot, humid summer weather can cause tornadoes. Minnesota is part of "Tornado Alley." It has more than 20 tornadoes every year.

Four states border Minnesota. North and South Dakota border it to the west. Iowa lies to the south and Wisconsin is to the east. The country of Canada is to the north. Lake Superior borders Minnesota in the northeast corner.

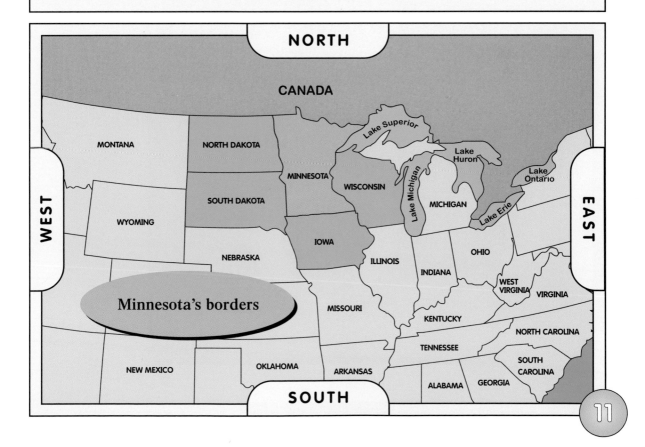

# Minnesota

**State abbreviation:** MN

**State nickname:** The Gopher State

**State capital:** St. Paul

**State motto:** *L'Etoile du Nord* (French for "The Star of the North")

**Statehood:** May 11, 1858, 32nd state

**Population:** 4,919,479, ranks 21st

**Land area:** 84,397 square miles (218,587 sq km), ranks 12th

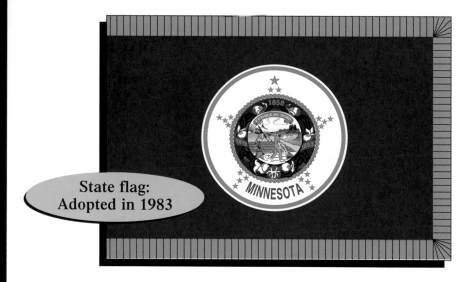

State flag: Adopted in 1983

**State song:** "Hail! Minnesota"

**State government:** Three branches: legislative, executive, and judicial

**Average July temperature:** 70°F (21°C)

**Average January temperature:** 8°F (-13°C)

State flower:
Pink and white lady's slipper

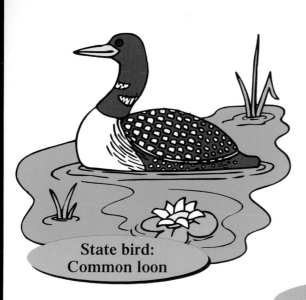

State bird:
Common loon

State tree:
Norway pine

# Cities And The Capital

St. Paul is the capital of Minnesota. It is the second-largest city in the state. St. Paul is located along the Mississippi River. St. Paul is very close to Minneapolis. Because of this, the two cities are often called the "Twin Cities."

The Capitol in St. Paul.

The skyline of Minneapolis.

Minneapolis is Minnesota's largest city. Minneapolis is famous for its skyways. The skyway is a system of walkways between downtown buildings. People can walk indoors. This keeps them warm during cold winter months.

# Famous Citizens

## Judy Garland (1922–1969)

Judy Garland was born in Grand Rapids in 1922. She was an actress and a singer. She starred in many musicals. Garland is most famous for playing Dorothy in *The Wizard of Oz*.

Judy Garland

# Famous Citizens

## Sinclair Lewis (1885–1951)

Sinclair Lewis was a famous writer. He was born in Sauk Centre in 1885. He is known for writing a novel called *Main Street* in 1920. It was written about his hometown in Minnesota. Also, he was the first American to win the Nobel Prize for literature. This happened in 1930.

Sinclair Lewis

# Fort Snelling

Fort Snelling sits on the bluff where the Mississippi and Minnesota rivers meet. The United States Army arrived and started building the fort in 1819. When the soldiers arrived, the land was wilderness. A few settlers and Native American tribes lived there. The fort was finished in 1825. It was named for Colonel Josiah Snelling.

By building the fort, the soldiers changed the area around the fort. They planted crops, built mills, and enforced laws. These changes attracted more settlers to the area. Soon people started getting supplies at the fort. Some people stayed there.

Fort Snelling

Fort Snelling was an active military base until the end of World War II. It became the state's first national historic landmark in 1960. Today, many people visit the museum at Fort Snelling. Some of Minnesota's oldest buildings are there. Guides dress up as soldiers. They teach people about the history of Fort Snelling.

# Lakes Of Minnesota

Minnesota is known as the "Land of 10,000 Lakes." But there are really more than 15,000 lakes around the state. Water covers more of Minnesota than any other state. More than 4,750 square miles (12,302 sq km) of Minnesota is covered by water.

This Minnesota lake is in Winona County.

There are many famous lakes in Minnesota. Lake Itasca is famous because it is where the Mississippi River starts. Red Lake is famous because it is Minnesota's largest lake. It measures 430 square miles (1,114 sq km).

In Minneapolis, there are five lakes called the Chain of Lakes. These are famous because they are connected to each other. Their names are Brownie Lake, Cedar Lake, Lake of the Isles, Lake Calhoun, and Lake Harriet. Many people swim, bike, and walk around these lakes.

Lake Harriet is part of
the Chain of Lakes.

One important lake in Minnesota is Lake Superior. Parts of Lake Superior are in Canada, Michigan, and Wisconsin, too. Lake Superior is the world's largest body of fresh water. The lake is an important port for ships because it connects to the Atlantic Ocean. Many people visit Lake Superior to see the scenery, and go boating or fishing. The water is usually too cold to go swimming, though.

# Mall Of America

The Mall of America opened in 1992. This mall is located in Bloomington. It is one of the top places in the United States for people to visit.

Minnesota is home to the Mall of America.

The Mall of America has more than 4 million square feet (371,612 sq m) of space. It is the largest mall in the United States.

(Above) People go on rides at Camp Snoopy.
(Below) The characters of Camp Snoopy.

The Mall of America has more than 520 stores. There are also restaurants, movie theaters, bowling alleys, and nightclubs. The mall also has a theme park with more than 30 rides. This is called Camp Snoopy. It also has an aquarium people can visit. This is called Underwater Adventures.

Sharks and other sea life can be seen at Underwater Adventures.

# Minnesota

**1660:** Two French fur traders arrive in Minnesota on Lake Superior.

**1803:** President Thomas Jefferson arranges for the United States to buy Minnesota in the Louisiana Purchase.

Lake Superior

**1858:** Minnesota becomes the 32nd state on May 11.

**1889:** The Mayo Clinic opens in Rochester.

**1927:** Charles Lindbergh Jr. of Little Falls flies across the Atlantic Ocean. He is the first person to fly alone and without stopping.

**1956:** Southdale Center opens in Edina. It is the first enclosed shopping mall in the United States.

**1963:** The Guthrie Theater opens in Minneapolis.

**1965:** Minnesota Senator Hubert H. Humphrey becomes vice president of the United States.

**1977:** Minnesota Senator Walter Mondale becomes vice president of the United States.

**1992:** The Mall of America opens in Bloomington.

**1999:** Former professional wrestler Jesse Ventura becomes governor.

**2002:** Senator Paul Wellstone dies in a plane crash.

Hubert Humphrey

# Cities In Minnesota

Red Lake

Grand Rapids

Moorhead

Duluth

Little Falls

Sauk Centre

St. Paul

Minneapolis

Edina

Bloomington

Rochester

# Important Words

capital  a city where government leaders meet.

humid  air that is damp or moist.

Louisiana Purchase  a deal where the United States bought land from France. Part of this land later became Minnesota.

nickname  a name that describes something special about a person or a place.

settler  a person who comes from another place and sets up a permanent residence.

tornado  a storm cloud that is shaped like a funnel and swirls fast, destroying homes and cities.

World War II  the second war between many countries that happened from 1939 to 1945.

# Web Sites

To learn more about Minnesota, visit ABDO Publishing Company on the World Wide Web. Web site links about Minnesota are featured on our Book Links page. These links are routinely monitored and updated to provide the most current information available.

www.abdopub.com

# Index